STRING BASS

Intermediate Scales and Bowings

for STRINGS

by HARVEY S. WHISTLER and HERMAN A. HUMMEL

CONTENTS

RUBANK®

HAL•LEONARD® CORPORATION
7777 W. BLUEMOUND RD. P.O. BOX 13819 MILWAUKEE, WI 53213

Key of C Major

Détaché Scale

1 

Use whole bow with détaché bowing.

Relative Minor Scales and Chords

2 

3 

Scales and Chords in Eighth Notes

4 

5 

6 

Staccato Scales

7 

8 

Scale and Chord in 6/8 Meter

9 

Triplets

10 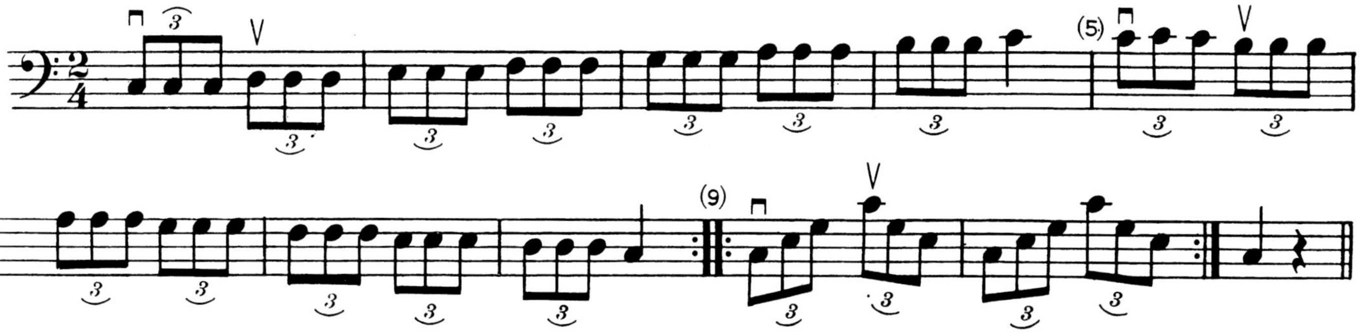

Dotted Eighth and Sixteenth Notes

11 

Be sure to start UP BOW. Play at extreme tip of stick, using about four inches of hair.

12 

Articulated Scales and Chords

13 

14 

15 

16 

Key of G Major

Détaché Scale

17

Use whole bow with détaché bowing.

Relative Minor Scales and Chords

18

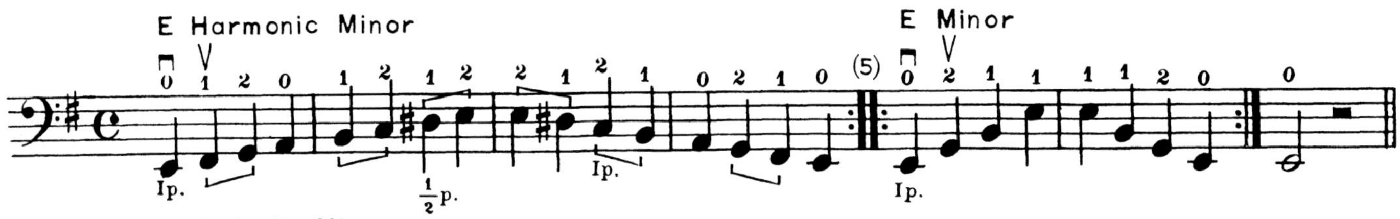

19

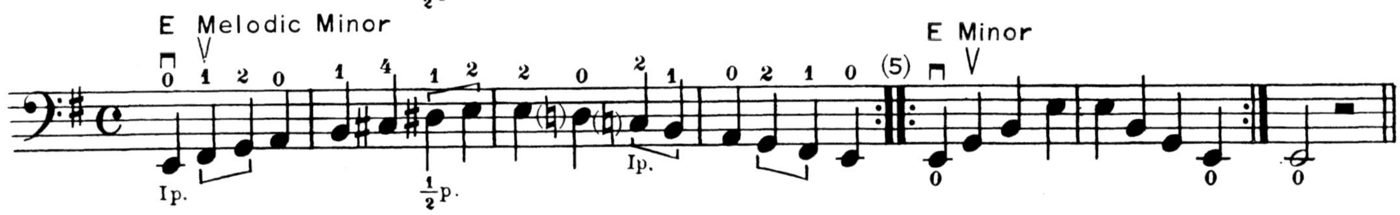

Scales and Chords in Eighth Notes

20

21

22

Staccato Scales

23

24

Scale and Chord in 6/8 Meter

25 

Triplets

26 

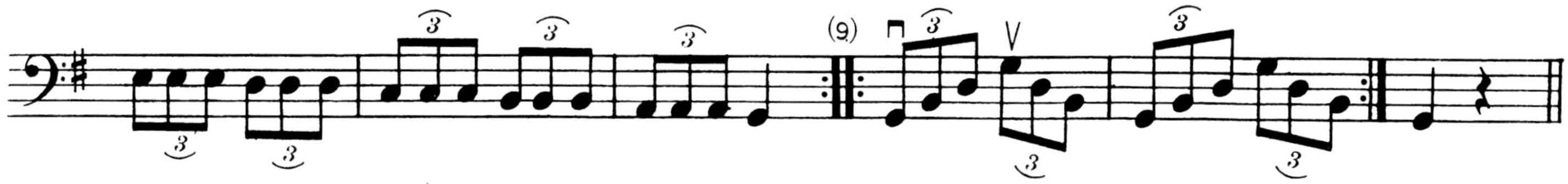

Dotted Eighth and Sixteenth Notes

27 

Be sure to start UP BOW. Play at extreme tip of stick, using about four inches of hair.

28 

Articulated Scales and Chords

29 

30 

31 

32 

Key of D Major

Détaché Scale

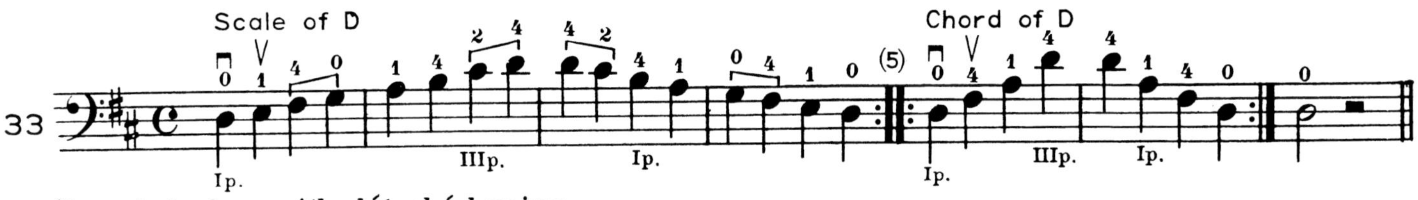

Use whole bow with détaché bowing.

Relative Minor Scales and Chords

Scales and Chords in Eighth Notes

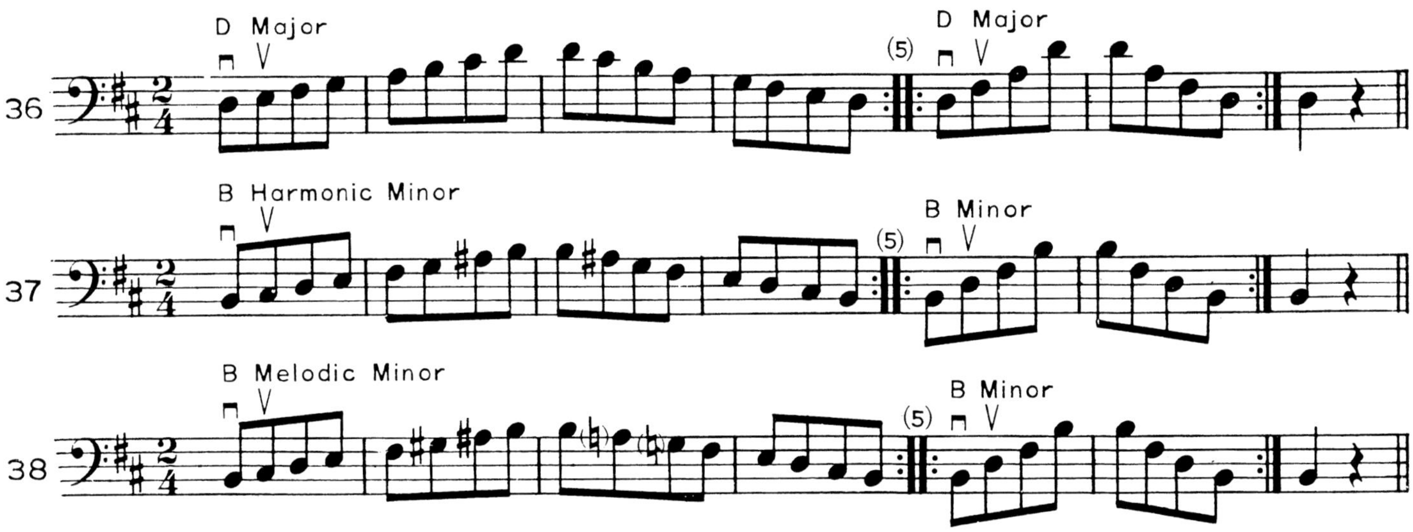

Staccato Scales

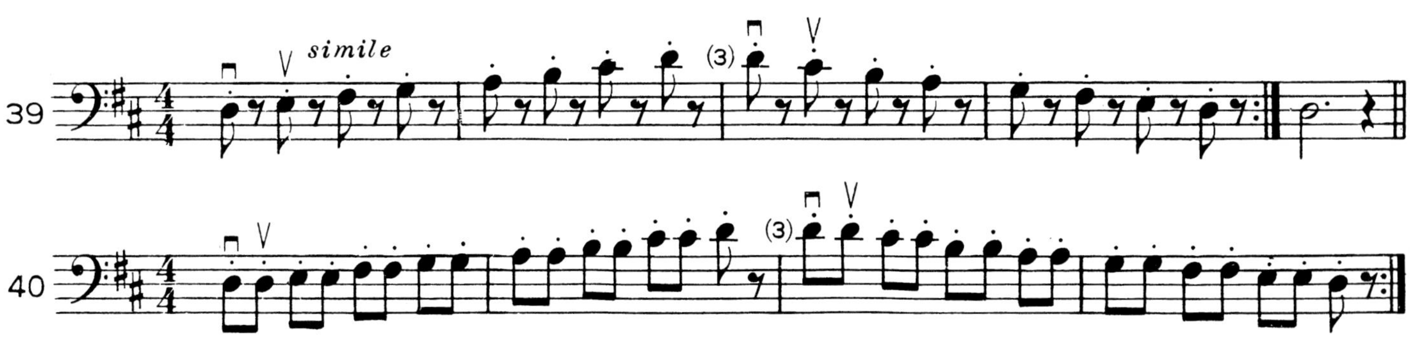

Scale and Chord in 6/8 Meter

41 

Triplets

42 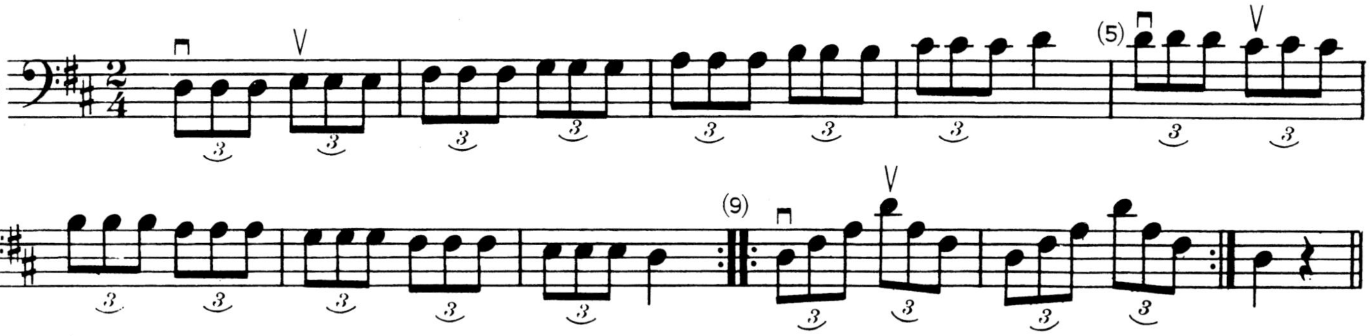

Dotted Eighth and Sixteenth Notes

43 

Be sure to start UP BOW. Play at extreme tip of stick, using about four inches of hair.

44 

Articulated Scales and Chords

45 

46 

47 

48 

Key of A Major

Détaché Scale

49 

Use whole bow with détaché bowing.

Relative Minor Scales and Chords

50 

51 

Scales and Chords in Eighth Notes

52 

53 

54 

Staccato Scales

55 

56 

Scale and Chord in 6/8 Meter

57

Triplets

58

Dotted Eighth and Sixteenth Notes

59

Be sure to start UP BOW. Play at extreme tip of stick, using about four inches of hair.

60

Articulated Scales and Chords

61

62

63

64

Key of F Major

Détaché Scale

65

Use whole bow with détaché bowing.

Relative Minor Scales and Chords

66
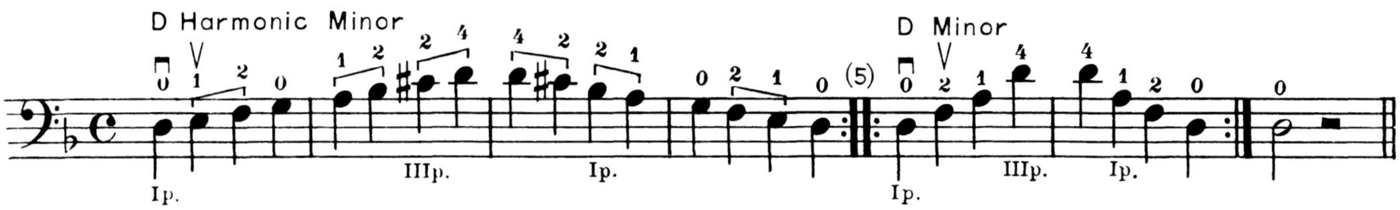

67
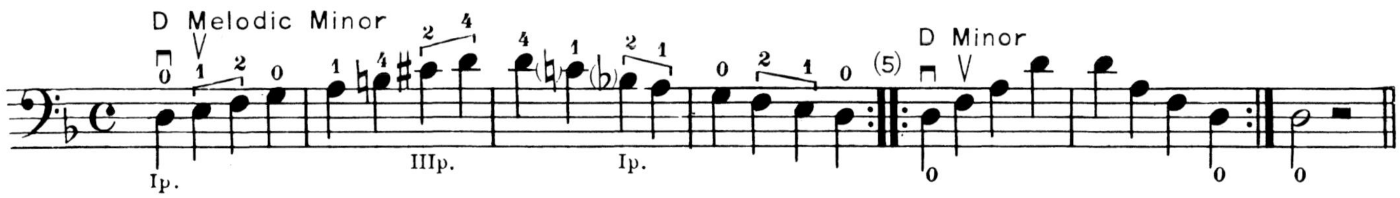

Scales and Chords in Eighth Notes

68

69

70

Staccato Scales

71

72

Scale and Chord in 6/8 Meter

73

Triplets

74
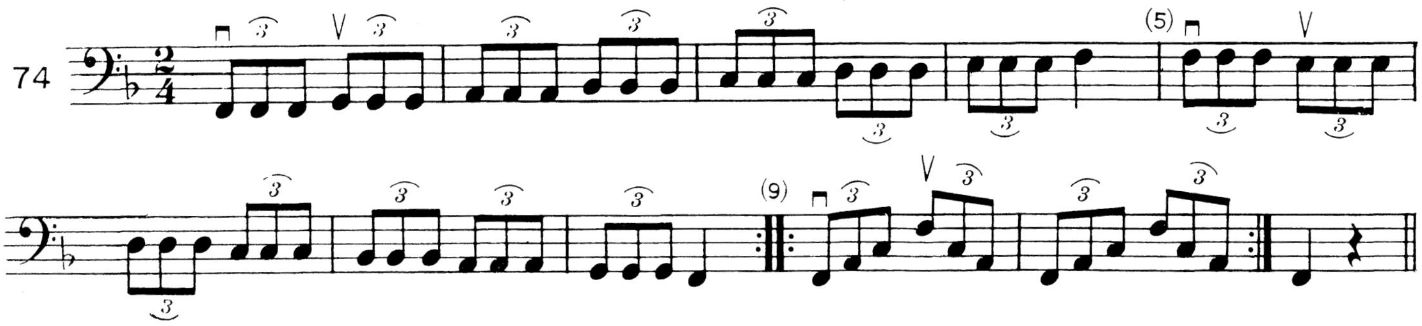

Dotted Eighth and Sixteenth Notes

75

Be sure to start UP BOW. Play at extreme tip of stick, using about four inches of hair.

76

Articulated Scales and Chords

77

78

79

80

Key of B♭ Major

Détaché Scale

81 

Use whole bow with détaché bowing.

Relative Minor Scales and Chords

82 

83 

Scales and Chords in Eighth Notes

84 

85 

86 

Staccato Scales

87 

88 

Scale and Chord in 6/8 Meter

89 

Triplets

90 

Dotted Eighth and Sixteenth Notes

91 

Be sure to start UP BOW. Play at extreme tip of stick, using about four inches of hair.

92 

Articulated Scales and Chords

93 

94 

95 

96 

Key of E♭ Major

Détaché Scale

97 

Use whole bow with détaché bowing.

Relative Minor Scales and Chords

98 

99 

Scales and Chords in Eighth Notes

100 

101 

102 

Staccato Scales

103 

104 

Scale and Chord in 6/8 Meter

105 

Triplets

106 

Dotted Eighth and Sixteenth Notes

107 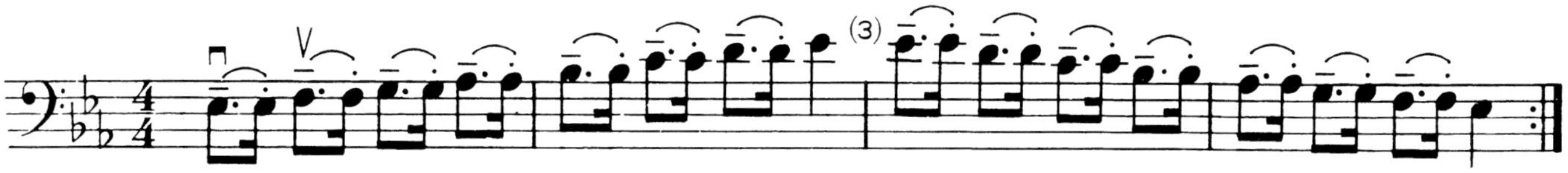

Be sure to start UP BOW. Play at extreme tip of stick, using about four inches of hair.

108 

Articulated Scales and Chords

109 

110 

111 

112 

Chromatic Scales

Extended Chromatic Scale

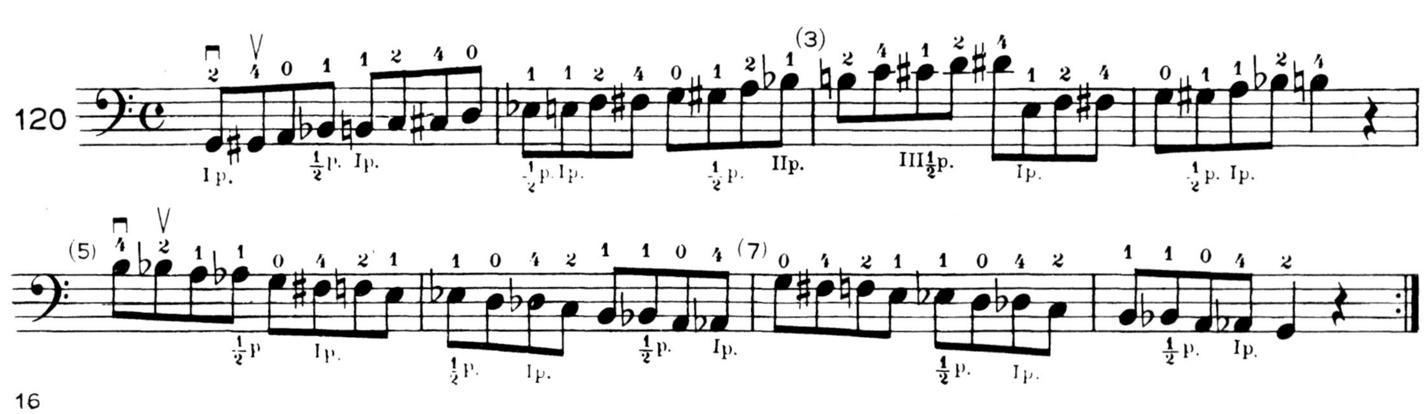